To Jon & Rose
Be inspired!

Iran Inspired

Steve
2008

Impressions of Iran
captured in quotations and drawings.

Steve Unwin

Photon Books
www.photonbooks.com

Published by Photon Books
First published in Great Britain in 2008
www.photonbooks.com

Printed and bound in Great Britain

ISBN   978-1-906420-07-9

ATEBIDIC4.0

Printed and bound in Great Britain
by Biddles Ltd, Kings Lynn
www.biddles.co.uk

Acknowledgements

It has been my great pleasure to visit Iran and meet some of its people. I am deeply grateful for the profound effects these visits have had on my thinking and my work on personal and organisational change.

There are many friends that I have made and I dedicate this book to all of them. I hope that even though it is not possible to name them individually, this book conveys a little of the thanks and gratitude I owe them.

I must thank the Iranian Society of Quality Managers and in particular there are two people who cannot remain unnamed; Mr Hesam Aref Kashfi and Mr. Hamid Saraidarian. I thank them both for their dedication, foresight and kindness which have made my wonderful experiences of Iran possible.

Steve Unwin
June 2008

ISⓆM

"Roam abroad in the world, and take thy fill of its enjoyments
before the day shall come when thou must quit it for good."
Saadi

Preface

I have been fortunate to have the opportunity to visit Iran several times to speak at the International Conference of Quality Managers, and this book aims to capture some of the experience of these visits and what they have meant to me.

A diary would capture the chronology of events, places visited and people met; the tangible evidence of the occasion. However I have learned that it is often in the space between these tangibles that the real value of an experience resides. In the connection between things, or the shadows they cast is where the magic can be found. The magic that changes our understanding and through this changes who we are. This after all is the essence of what an experience is. It is the footprint the beach leaves on us that matters, not those we leave on the beach.

But to capture the space between things is not easy. As soon as it is described it ceases to be a space and becomes a thing itself.

In addressing this challenge I have in mind one of my young daughter's dot-to-dot puzzles. I have provided quotations to represent the dots and drawings that invoke the experience. You are now invited to join these dots to create your own unique pictures that will exist nowhere but within you and will of course change as you change. My hope is that these pictures provide new insights and energy for your own journey of change.

I wish you 'Bon Voyage' on your journey.

If you would like to share your comments and thoughts I would love to hear from you.

Please email iran@photonbooks.com.

"The minute you begin to do what you want to do, it's a different kind of life."
Buckminster Fuller

Changed Perspectives

It is a paradox that we live in a world where the pace of change grows by the day. Technology allows us to travel the world, yet the world we find on our travels looks increasingly like the home we left behind. What was once diverse, increasingly looks and feels the same.

There are aspects to this uniformity that are very welcome. My travels have confirmed, that we are all indeed the same. Within each of us are the same needs, the same desires, fears and ambitions. There is a common thread in who we are, whatever our nationality or culture.

However as we face the challenges of change we also need to value differences.; being able to perceive things differently, draw alternate conclusions, connect concepts in innovative ways.

A joy of my visits to Iran is this combination of sameness and diversity, a sharing of who we are, but differences in what that means, how we see, act and understand.

The sameness brings us together with a common human bond. and the diversity gives us a richness of things to share.

The ICQM annually brings together 5000 people from across the world to share experiences, ideas, discoveries, challenges and much more in an atmosphere of kinship.

I hope here to have captured something of my experience of Iran in ways that allow us to recognise and celebrate what makes each of us the same and what makes each of us different.

Iran Inspired

Tehran Tehran

"Discovery consists of looking at the same thing as everyone else does and thinking something different."
Albert Szent-Györgyi

"Most people are mirrors, reflecting the moods and emotions of the times; few are windows, bringing light to bear on the dark corners where troubles fester. The whole purpose of education is to turn mirrors into windows."
Sydney J. Harris

"To the artist is sometimes granted a sudden, transient insight... A flash, and where previously the brain held a dead fact, the soul grasps a living truth!"
Arnold Bennett

"I would sooner live in a cottage and wonder at everything than live in a castle and wonder at nothing!"
Joan Winmill Brown

"He is rich or poor according to what he is, not according to what he has."
Henry Ward Beecher

"Have less, do less. Be more."
Aboodi Shaby

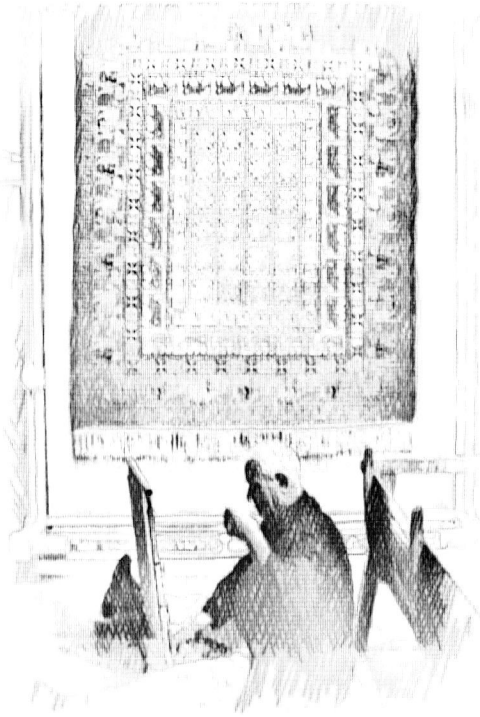

"A weaver who has to direct and to interweave a great many little threads has no time to philosophize about it, rather, he is so absorbed in his work that he doesn't think, he acts: and it's nothing he can explain, he just feels how things should go."
Vincent Van Gogh

"Every man's work, whether it be literature or music or pictures or architecture or anything else is always a portrait of himself."
Samuel Butler

"Though we seem to be sleeping, there is an inner wakefulness that directs the dream, and that will eventually startle us back to the truth of who we are."
Rumi

"Courage is the greatest of all the virtues. Because if you haven't courage, you may not have an opportunity to use any of the others."
Samuel Johnson

"It takes an uncommon amount of guts to put your dreams on the line, to hold them up and say, 'How good or bad am I?' That's where the courage comes in."
Erma Bombeck

"To avoid criticism do nothing, say nothing, be nothing."
Elbert Hubbard

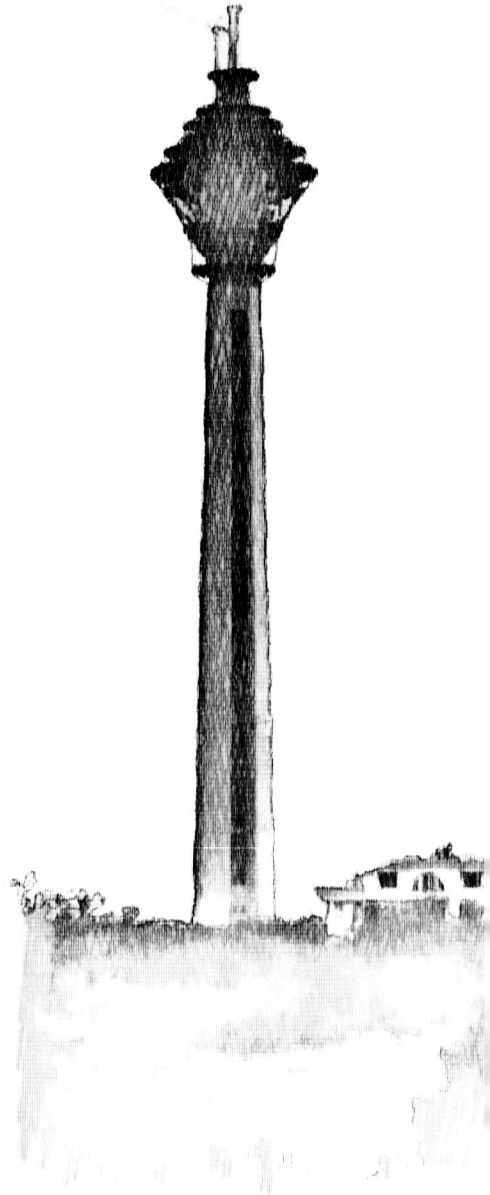

"Wear a smile and have friends; wear a scowl and have wrinkles. What do we live for if not to make the world less difficult for each other?"
George Eliot

"The ultimate reason for setting goals is to entice you to become the person it takes to achieve them."
Jim Rohn

"Whosoever wishes to know about the world
must learn about it in its particular details.
Knowledge is not intelligence.
In searching for the truth be ready for the
unexpected.
Change alone is unchanging.
The same road goes both up and down.
The beginning of a circle is also its end.
Not I, but the world says it: all is one.
And yet everything comes in season."
Heracleitus of Ephesos

"Only one-in-a-million will strive with full intent and courage to become the unique somebody that person was created and destined to be! And yet each of us was destined at birth to be a one-in-a-million person!"
Dr. William Mitchell

"There is no such thing as a 'self-made' man. We are made up of thousands of others. Everyone who has ever done a kind deed for us, or spoken one word of encouragement to us, has entered into the make-up of our character and of our thoughts, as well as our success."
George Burton Adams

"In oneself lies the whole world and if you know how to look and learn then the door is there and the key is in your hand. Nobody on earth can give you either the key or the door to open, except yourself."
Jiddu Krishnamurti

"Have faith
and pursue the
unknown
end."
Oliver Wendell
Holmes, Jr.

"Without great solitude no serious work is possible."
Pablo Picasso

"We live in a rainbow of chaos."
Paul Cezanne

"Every man who is truly a man must learn to be alone in the midst of all others, and if need be against all others."
Romain Rolland.

The Conference The Conference

"If you have an apple and I have an apple and we exchange these apples then you and I will still each have one apple. But if you have an idea and I have an idea and we exchange these ideas, then each of us will have two ideas."
George Bernard Shaw

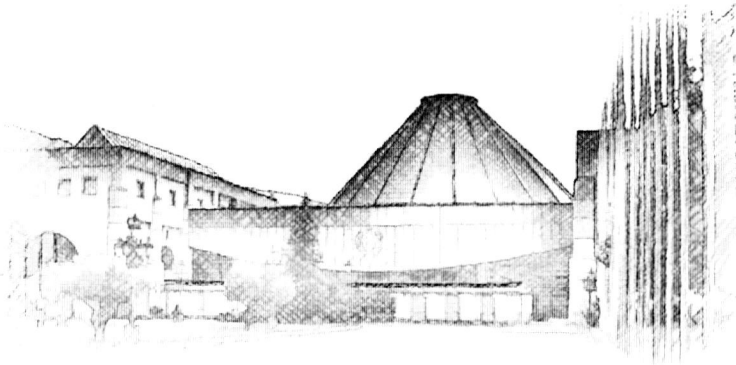

"If you risk nothing, then you risk everything."
Geena Davis

"He who possesses the source of enthusiasm will achieve great things. Doubt not. You will gather friends around you As a hair clasp gathers the hair."
I Ching

"Craziness is doing the same thing and expecting a different result."
Tom DeMarco

"If you were all alone in the universe with no one to talk to, no one with which to share the beauty of the stars, to laugh with, to touch, what would be your purpose in life? It is other life, it is love, which gives your life meaning. This is harmony. We must discover the joy of each other, the joy of challenge, the joy of growth."
Mitsugi Saotome

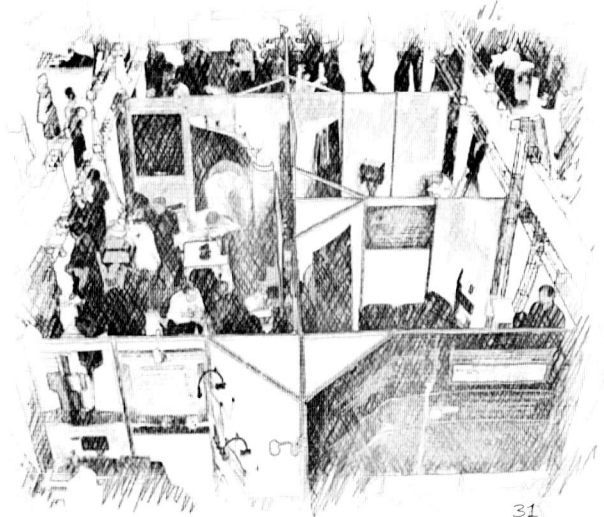

"A teacher affects eternity; he can never tell where his influence stops."
Henry Adams

"Some fragrance remains on the hand that gives the roses."
Chinese Proverb

"Successful communication transforms your thoughts, will, and desire into action. It moves people. It transforms the thoughts, will and desires of others. What better word for this process than magic?"
Jack Griffin

"We should be as careful of the books we read, as of the company we keep. The dead very often have more power than the living."
Tryon Edwards

"I think we ought to read only the kind of books that wound and stab us."
Franz Kafka

"What you leave behind is not what is engraved in stone monuments, but what is woven into the lives of others."
Pericles

"A mighty flame followeth a tiny spark."
Dante

"Be daring, be different, be impractical, ...

... be anything that will assert integrity of purpose and imaginative vision against the play-it-safers, the creatures of the commonplace, the slaves of the ordinary."
Cecil Beaton

"It takes one a long time to become young."
Pablo Picasso

"It is very easy to overestimate the importance of our own achievements in comparison with what we owe others."
Dietrich Bonhoeffer

"Unity is not something we are called to create; it's something we are called to recognize."
William Sloane Coffin

"You can't help getting older, but you don't have to get old."
George Burns

Isfahan & Shiraz

"Yesterday is ashes;
tomorrow wood. Only
today does the fire
burn brightly."
Eskimo proverb

"Education either functions as an instrument which is used to facilitate integration of the younger generation into the logic of the present system and bring about conformity...

...or it becomes the practice of freedom, the means by which men and women deal critically and creatively with reality and discover how to participate in the transformation of their world."

Paulo Freire

"Those things that nature denied to human sight, she revealed to the eyes of the soul."
Ovid

"Work is either fun or drudgery.
It depends on your attitude.
I like fun."
Colleen C. Barrett

"When I stand before God at the end of my life, I would hope
that I would not have a single bit of talent left, and could say,
'I used everything you gave me.'"
Erma Bombeck

"I wanted a perfect ending. Now I've learned, the hard way, that some poems don't rhyme, and some stories don't have a clear beginning, middle, and end. Life is about not knowing, having to change, taking the moment and making the best of it, without knowing what's going to happen next. Delicious ambiguity." Gilda Radner

"What is it you plan to do with your one wild and precious life?"
Mary Oliver

"The happiest people are those who think the most interesting thoughts. Those who decide to use leisure as a means of mental development, who love good music, good books, good pictures, good company, good conversation, are the happiest people in the world. And they are not only happy in themselves, they are the cause of happiness in others."
William Lyon Phelps

"Only in quiet waters things mirror themselves undistorted,
Only in quiet mind is adequate perception of the world."
Hans Margolius.

"Reach high, for stars lie hidden in your soul. Dream deep, for every dream precedes the goal."
Pamela Vaull Starr

"The problems of the world cannot possibly be solved by skeptics or cynics whose horizons are limited by the obvious realities. We need men who can dream of things that never were."
John Fitzgerald Kennedy

"The greatest good you can do for another is not just to share your riches but to reveal to him his own."
Benjamin Disraeli

"The illusion that we are separate from one another is an optical delusion of our consciousness."
Albert Einstein

"It's not so much that we're afraid of change or so in love with the old ways, but it's that place in between that we fear ...

... It's like being between trapezes. It's Linus when his blanket is in the dryer. There's nothing to hold on to."
Marilyn Ferguson

"Trust that little voice in your head that says "Wouldn't it be interesting if.."; And then do it."
Duane Michals

"As soon as you trust yourself, you will know how to live."
Garth Henrichs

"Your imagination has much to do with your life....It is for you to decide how you want your imagination to serve you."
Philip Conley

"The weakest among us
has a gift, however
seemingly trivial, which
is peculiar to him, and
which worthily used, will
be a gift also to his race."
John Ruskin

"Don't aim at success -- the more you aim at it and make it a target, the more you are going to miss it. For success, like happiness, cannot be pursued; it must ensue. . as the unintended side-effect of one's personal dedication to a course greater that oneself."
Victor Frankl

"If you're still hanging onto a dead dream of yesterday, laying flowers on its grave by the hour, you cannot be planting the seeds for a new dream to grow today."
Joyce Chapman

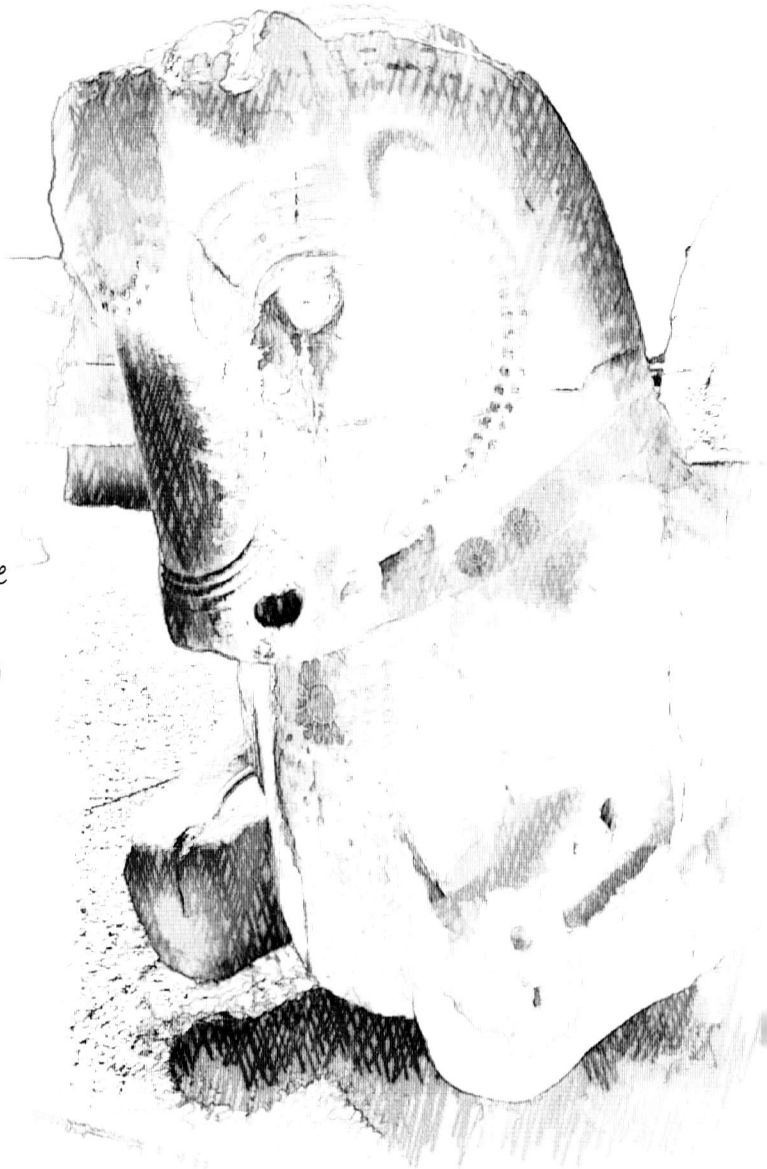

"You aren't your experiences. You are what you make of them."
Deborah Bell

"Man's main task in life is to give birth to himself."
Erich Fromm

"Ideas shape the course of history."
John Maynard Keynes

"Happy are those who dream dreams and are ready to pay the price to make them come true."
L.J. Cardinal Suenens

"No one is less ready for tomorrow than the person who holds the most rigid beliefs about what tomorrow will contain."
Jim Taylor

"There is a great man who makes every man feel small. But the real great man is the man who makes every man feel great."
G.K. Chesterton

"We rely upon the poets, the philosophers and the playwrights to articulate what most of us can only feel, in joy or sorrow. They illuminate the thoughts for which we only grope. They give us the strength and balm we cannot find in ourselves. Whenever I find my courage wavering I rush to them. They give me the wisdom of acceptance, the will and resilience to push on."
Helen Hayes

"I would rather have
a mind opened by
wonder than one
closed by belief."
Gerry Spence

"The power of the world always works in circles, and everything tries to be round. The sky is round, and I have heard that the earth is like a ball, and so are all the stars. The wind, in its greatest power, whirls; birds make their nests in circles, for theirs is the same religion as ours. The sun and moon, both round, come forth and go down again in a circle. Even the seasons form a great circle in their changing, and always come back again to where they were. The life of a person is a circle from childhood to childhood, and so it is in everything where power moves."

Black Elk

Yazd **Yazd**

"When I was a young man, I wanted to change the world. I found it was difficult to change the world, so I tried to change my nation. When I found I couldn't change the nation, I began to focus on my town. I couldn't change the town and as an older man, I tried to change my family. Now, as an old man, I realize the only thing I can change is myself, and suddenly I realize that if long ago I had changed myself, I could have made an impact on my family. My family and I could have made an impact on our town. Their impact could have changed the nation and I could indeed have changed the world."
Author Unknown

"If not you, then who? If not now, then when?"
Hillel

"Sometimes you just have to take the leap,
and build your wings on the way down."

Kobi Yamada

"Thus, the task is, not so much to see what no one has yet seen; but to think what nobody has yet thought, about that which everybody sees."
Erwin Schrödinger

"Have you seen any fairies lately?~~ I asked the question of a little girl not long ago.~~ 'Huh! There's no such thing as fairies', she replied.~~ In some way the answer hurt me, and I have been vaguely disquieted when I have thought of it ever since.~~ Have you seen any fairies lately, or have you allowed the harsher facts of life to dull your 'seeing eye?'"
Laura Ingalls Wilder

"Miracles happen to those who believe in them."
Bernard Berenson

"You're going to have to find out where you want to go. And then you've got to start going there. But immediately. You can't afford to lose a minute."
J. D. Salinger

"I have always been delighted at the prospect of a new day, a fresh try, one more start, with perhaps a bit of magic waiting somewhere behind the morning."
J. B. Priestley

"With too much data, too many demands, and too much competition, is it any wonder that people today are looking for ways to stop and smell the roses?"
Nick Campbell

"If a man is called to be a street sweeper, he should sweep streets even as Michelangelo painted, or Beethoven played music, or Shakespeare wrote poetry. He should sweep streets so well that all the hosts of heaven and earth will pause to say, here lived a great street sweeper who did his job well."
Martin Luther King

"The human heart feels things the eyes cannot see, and knows what the mind cannot understand."
Robert Vallett

"Discoveries
are often
made by not
following
instructions,
by going off
the main
road, by
trying the
untried."
Frank Tyger

"I learn by going
where I have to go."
Theodore Roethke

"What you will do
matters. All you
need is to do it."
Judy Grahn

"Your mind knows only some things. Your inner voice, your instinct, knows everything. If you listen to what you know instinctively, it will always lead you down the right path."
Henry Winkler

"The first step toward success is taken when you refuse to be a captive of the environment in which you first find yourself."
Mark Caine

"Simplicity is the ultimate sophistication."
Leonardo da Vinci

"Success is living up to your potential. That's all.
Wake up with a smile and go after life ...

...Live it, enjoy it, taste it, smell it, feel it."
Joe Kapp

"To finish the moment, to find the journey's end in every step of the road, to live the greatest number of good hours, is wisdom."
Ralph Waldo Emerson

"The great man is he that does not lose his child's heart."
Mencius

"Be soft in your practice. Think of the method as a fine silvery stream, not a raging waterfall. Follow the stream, have faith in its course. It will go its own way, meandering here, trickling there. It will find the grooves, the cracks, the crevices. Just follow it. Never let it out of your sight. It will take you."
Sheng-Yen

"Be humble, for you are made of dung.
Be noble, for you are made of stars."
Serbian proverb

"Adventures
don't begin
until you step
into the
forest. That
first step in
an act of
faith."
Mickey Hart

"Risk is essential. There is not growth of inspiration in staying within what is safe and comfortable. Once you find out what you do best, why not try something else?"
Alex Noble

"Normally,
we do not so
much as
look at
things as
overlook
them."
Alan Watts

"A rock pile ceases to be a rock pile the moment a single man contemplates it, bearing within him the image of a cathedral."
Antoine de Saint-Exupery

SILK ROAD HOTEL

"A table, a chair, a bowl of fruit and a violin; what else does a man need to be happy?"
Albert Einstein

"When you are inspired by some great purpose, some extraordinary project, all of your thoughts break their bonds: your mind transcends limitations, your consciousness expands in every direction and you find yourself in a new, great, and wonderful world. Dormant forces, faculties and talents become alive and you discover yourself to be a greater person than you ever dreamed yourself to be." Patanjali.

"What we imagine is order is merely the prevailing form of chaos."
Kerry Thornley

"Divisions are imaginary lines drawn by small minds."
Paramhansa Yogananda

"My movie is born first in my head,
dies on paper;
is resuscitated by the living persons and real objects I use,
which are killed on film but,
placed in a certain order and projected on to a screen, come to life again like flowers in water."
Robert Bresson

"Rules and models destroy genius and art."
William Hazlitt

"To write it, it took three months; to conceive it -- three minutes; to collect the data in it -- all my life."
F. Scott Fitzgerald

"Great poetry is always written by somebody straining to go beyond what he can do."
Sir Stephen Spender:

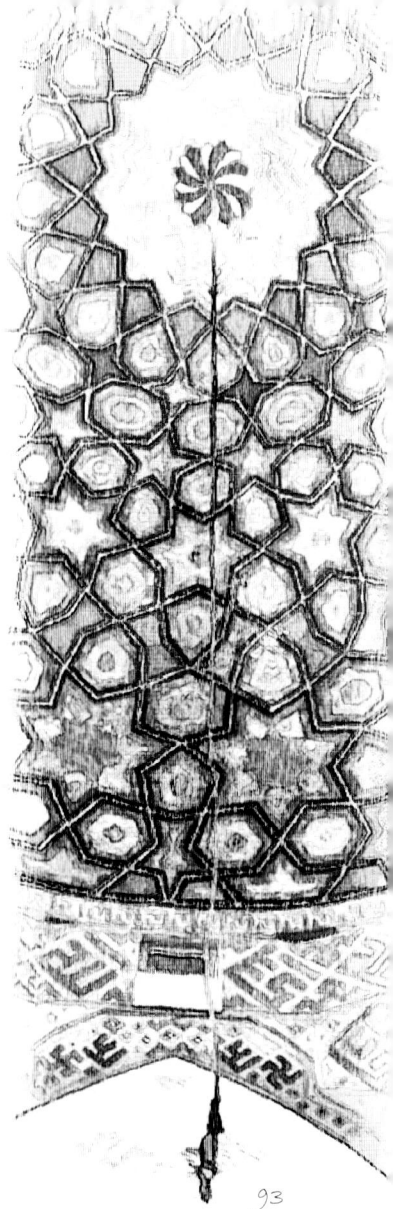

"One's destination is never a place,...

...but rather a new way of looking at things."
Henry Miller

"When the well's dry, we know the worth of water."
Benjamin Franklin

"The person who can combine frames of reference and draw connections between ostensibly unrelated points of view is likely to be the one who makes the creative breakthrough."
Denise Shekerjian

"Judging by what I have learned about men and women, I am convinced that far more idealistic aspiration exists than is ever evident. Just as the rivers we see are much less numerous than the underground streams, so the idealism that is visible is minor compared to what men and women carry in their hearts, unreleased or scarcely released. Mankind is waiting and longing for those who can accomplish the task of untying what is knotted and bringing the underground waters to the surface."
Albert Schweitzer

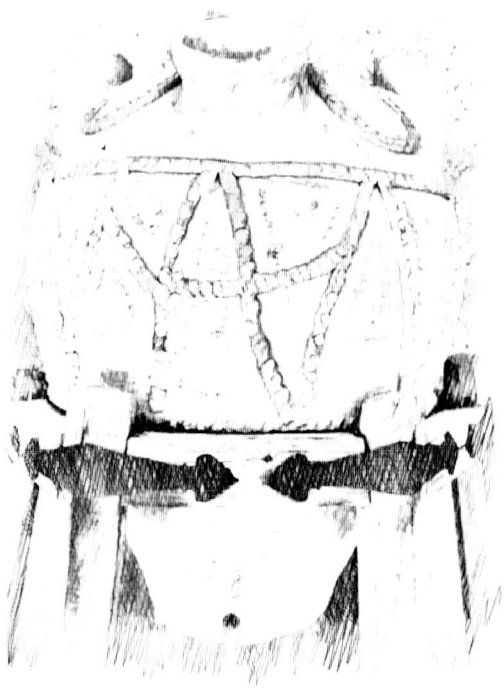

"One must
still have
chaos in
oneself to
give birth to
a dancing
star."
Friedrich
Nietzsche

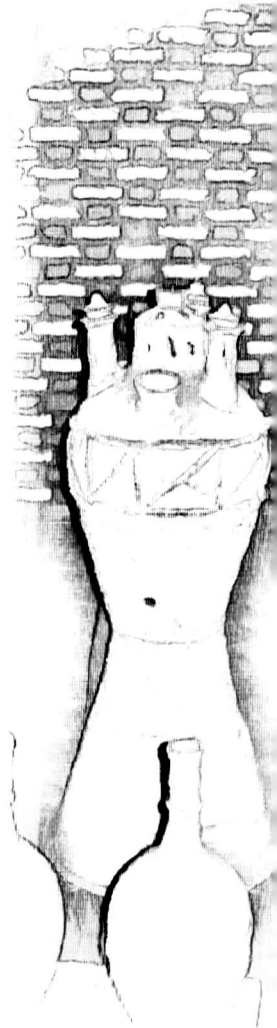

"Two roads diverged in a
wood, and I--
I took the one less
travelled by,
And that has made all
the difference."
Robert Frost

"I learned ... that inspiration does not come like a bolt, nor is it kinetic, energetic striving, but it comes into us slowly and quietly and all the time, though we must regularly and every day give it a little chance to start flowing, prime it with a little solitude and idleness."
Brenda Ueland

"Pack lightly and carry a compass."
Raul Fernandez

"Every moment of one's existence one is growing into more or retreating into less. One is always living a little more or dying a little bit."
Norman Mailer

"Everything you can imagine is real."
Pablo Picasso

"Dreams are today's answers to tomorrow's questions."
Edgar Cayce

"Travellers, there is no path,
paths are made by walking."
Antonio Machado

"It is not the answer that enlightens,
but the question."
Eugene Ionesco

"We see things not as they are...

...but as we are."
Anaïs Nin

"We see the brightness of a new page where everything yet can happen."
Rainer Maria Rilke

"There is a way that nature speaks, that land speaks. Most of the time we are simply not patient enough, quiet enough, to pay attention to the story."
Linda Hogan

"I never wear a watch, because I always know it's now -- and now is when you should do it."
Steve Mariucci

"All things change, nothing is extinguished. There is nothing in the whole world which is permanent. Everything flows onward; all things are brought into being with a changing nature; the ages themselves glide by in constant movement."
Ovid

"The timid and the fainthearted and people who expect quick results are doomed to disappointment."
Joseph Juran

Contributors

Adams, George Burton
Quoted on page 22

Adams, Henry Brooks (1838 - 1918)
Novelist historian, journalist and academic. Best known for his autobiographical work, 'The Education of Henry Adams'.
Quoted on page 32

Barrett, Colleen C. (Born 1944)
President and Chief Operating Officer, Southwest Airlines
Quoted on page 42

Beaton, Sir Cecil, Walter, Hardy (1904 - 1980)
English fashion and portrait photographer and stage costume designer for film and theatre.
Quoted on page 35

Beecher, Henry Ward (1813 - 1887)
Theologically liberal clergyman, social reformer abolitionist and speaker.
Quoted on page 14

Bell, Deborah
Ed. D. Boston University
Quoted on page 57

Bennett, Arnold (1867 - 1913)
British novelist. Author of the Clayhanger Trilogy and The Old Wives' Tale.
Quoted on page 13

Berenson, Bernard (1865 - 1959)
Lithuanian born American art critic.
Quoted on page 70

Black Elk (1863 - 1950)
Holy man of the Oglala Lakota (Sioux) native Indian tribe.
Quoted on page 65

Bombeck, Erma (1927 - 1996)
American humorist with popular newspaper column
Quoted on pages 18 & 43

Bonhoeffer, Deitrich (1906 - 1945)
German Lutheran pastor, theologian, member of the German Resistance Movement and founder member of the Confessing Church.
Quoted on page 36

Bresson, Robert (1901— 1999)
French film director known for his spiritual and ascetic style.
Quoted on page 92

Brown, Joan Winmill
Author and actress.
Quoted on page 14

Burns, George (1896 - 1996)
Academy Award winning comedian, actor and writer.
Quoted on page 37

Butler, Samuel (1835 - 1902)
British writer influenced by experience of New Zealand and best known for his utopian satire 'Erewhon'.
Quoted on page 16

Caine, Mark
Quoted on page 79

Campbell, Nick (Born 1952)
Canadian actor and filmmaker.
Quoted on page 73

Cayce, Edgar (1877 - 1945)
Celebrated psychic.
Quoted on page 103

Cezanne, Paul (1839 - 1906)
French artist and post-impressionist painter.
Quoted on page 26

Chapman, Joyce
Speaker and coach
Quoted on page 56

Chesterton, G.K. Gilbert Keith (1874 - 1936)
Prolific and diverse writer in areas including journalism, philosophy, poetry and biography.
Quoted on page 62

Chinese proverb
Quoted on page 32

Coffin, William Sloane (1924 - 2006)
Liberal Christian clergyman and peace activist.
Quoted on page 37

Conley, Philip
Quoted on page 53

Dante (1265 - 1321)
Italian poet. Author of The Devine Comedy.
Quoted on page 34

Da Vinci, Leonardo (1452 - 1519)
Italian polymath; scientist mathematician, engineer, inventor, anatomist, painter, sculptor, architect, botanist, musician and writer.
Quoted on page 80

Davis, Gena Virginia Elizabeth (Born 1956)
Academy and Golden Globe Award winning actress and former model.
Quoted on page 30

DeMarco, Tom
Author, speaker and teacher on software engineering topics.
Quoted on page 30

Disraeli, Benjamin (1804 - 1881)
First Earl of Beaconsfield. British statesman, Prime Minister and founder of the modern UK conservative party.
Quoted on page 49

Edwards, Tryon (1809 - 1894)
Theologian and author of the New Dictionary of Thoughts.
Quoted on page 33

Einstein, Albert 1979—1955

German born theoretical physicist. Best known for his theory of relativity, more specifically the mass-energy equivalence. $E=mc^2$. Nobel prize for physics

Quoted on pages 50 & 89

Eliot, George Mary Anne Evans (1819 - 1880)

Leading English novelist of the Victorian era. Author of 'the Mill on the Floss' and 'Middlemarch'.

Quoted on page 19

Emerson, Ralph Waldo 1803—1882

American essayist, poet, philosopher and leader of the transcendentalist movement.

Quoted on page 82

Eskimo proverb

Quoted on page 39

Ferguson, Marilyn (Born 1938)

World renown author public speaker and science communicator

Quoted on page 51

Fernandez, Raul

Entrepreneur, Chairman and CEO of ObjectVideo.

Quoted on page 101

Fitzgerald, F. Scott (1896 - 1940)

American writer of novels and short stories.

Quoted on page 93

Frankl, Viktor, Emil. (1905—1997)

Austrian neurologist, psychiatrist and holocaust survivor. Quotation from Man's Search for Meaning.

Quoted on page 55

Franklin, Benjamin (1706—1790)
US Author, painter, satirist, political theorist scientist, inventor and statesman
Quoted on page 95

Freire, Paulo (1921 - 1997)
Brazilian educator and theorist on education.
Quoted on page 40

Fromm, Erich (1900 - 1980)
Jewish-German-American social psychologist, psychoanalyst and humanistic philosopher.
Quoted on page 58

Frost, Robert (1871 - 1963)
Quadruple Pulitzer Prize winning poet of complex social and philosophical themes.
Quoted on page 99

Fuller, Richard **Buckminster** 'Bucky' (1895 - 1983)
American visionary, engineer, designer, architect, poet, author and inventor.
Quoted on page 6

Grahn, Judy
Poet and women centred cultural theorist.
Quoted on page 77

Griffin, Jack
Quoted on page 32

Harris, Sydney J. (1917 - 1986)
London born American newspaper journalist.
Quoted on page 12

Hart, Mickey
Percussionist and musicologist.
Quoted on page 85

Hayes, Helen (1900 - 1993)
Academy Award winning actress.
Quoted on page 63

Hazlitt, William (1778 - 1830)
English writer known for his humanistic essays. Often seen as the greatest literary critic after Samuel Johnson.
Quoted on page 93

Henrichs, Garth
Quoted on page 52

Heracleitus of Ephesos (535 - 475)
Pre-Socratic Greek philosopher.
Quoted on page 21

Hillel
Babylonian sage
Quoted on page 67

Hogan, Linda (Born 1947)
Native American poet, storyteller, academic, playwright, novelist, environmentalist and short story writer.
Quoted on page 107

Holmes, Oliver Wendell Jr. (1841 - 1935)
American jurist who served on the US Supreme Court.
Quoted on page 24

Hubbard, Elbert (1856 - 1915)
American writer, publisher, philosopher and artist.
Quoted on page 18

I Ching
Quoted on page 30

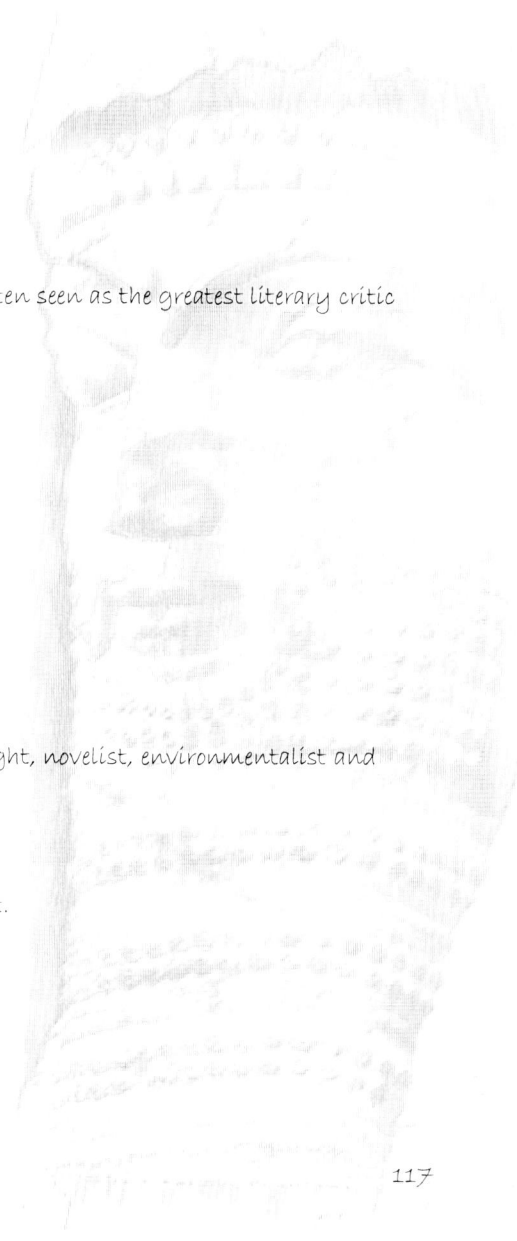

Ionesco, Eugene (1909 - 1994)
Playwright and dramatist. One of the foremost playwright of the Theatre of the Absurd.
Quoted on page 104

Johnson, Dr. Samuel (1709 - 1784)
English poet, essayist, biographer, lexicographer and critic of English literature. Well known for his aphorisms.
Quoted on page 18

Juran, Joseph (1904 - 2008)
Management consultant and evangelist for quality and quality management.
Quoted on page 110

Kafka, Franz (1883 - 1924)
Influential German language fiction writer.
Quoted on page 33

Kapp, Joe (Born 1938)
Professional US Football player.
Quoted on page 81

Kennedy, John Fitzgerald 1917—1963
35th president of the United States of America.
Quoted on page 48

Keynes, John Maynard (1883 - 1946)
British economist and major influence on economic and political theory.
Quoted on page 59

King, Martin Luther, Jr 1929—1968
Civil rights leader, political activist and Baptist minister. Regarded as one of America's finest orators, remembered for his 'I have a dream' speech. Youngest winner of the Nobel Peace Prize.
Quoted on page 74

Krishnamurti, Jiddu (1895—1986)
Indian Hindu philosopher, writer and spiritual speaker.
Quoted on page 23

Machado, Antonio (1875 - 1939)
Spanish poet and leading figure of the Spanish literary movement known as the
Generation of 98.
Quoted on page 104

Mailer, Norman (Born 1923)
Novelist, journalist, playwright, screenwriter and film director. Double Pulitzer Prize
winner.
Quoted on page 102

Margolius, Hans
Quoted on page 47

Mariucci, Steve (Born 1955)
US National football league coach.
Quoted on page 108

Mencius (372 - 289 BCE)
Chinese Confucian philosopher.
Quoted on page 83

Michals, Duane (Born 1932)
Innovative and artistic self-taught photographer who used photography and text to explore
emotion and philosophy.
Quoted on page 52

Mitchell, Dr. William
Quoted on page 22

Miller, Henry (1891 - 1980)
American writer and painter. Developed a new form of writing which incorporated autobiography, social criticism, philosophical reflection, surrealist free association and mysticism.
Quoted on page 94

Nietzsche, Friedrich (1844 - 1900)
Philosopher whose writing included critiques of religion, morality, contemporary culture, philosophy and science.
Quoted on page 98

Nin, Anaïs (1903 - 1977)
French born author who became famous for her published journals spanning 50 years.
Quoted on page 105

Noble, Alex
Quoted on page 86

Oliver, Mary (Born 1935)
American poet.
Quoted on page 45

Ovid (43 BC - 17 AD)
Roman poet. One of the three canonical poets of Latin literature.
Quoted on pages 41 & 109

Patanjali
Indian philosopher
Quoted on page 90

Pericles (495 - 429 BC)
Prominent statesman, orator and general of Athens.
Quoted on page 34

Phelps, William Lyon (1865 - 1943)
Author, critic and scholar.
Quoted on page 46

Picasso, Pablo (1881 - 1973)
One of the most recognised figures in 20th century western art. Co-founder of cubism.
Quoted on pages 25, 36 & 103

Priestly, J.B. (1894 - 1994)
English writer and broadcaster.
Quoted on page 72

Radner, Gilder Susan (1946 - 1989)
American comedienne and actress.
Quoted on page 44

Rilke, Rainer, Maria (1875 - 1926)
One of the German language's greatest poets of the 20th century.
Quoted on page 106

Roethke, Theodore (1908 - 1963)
Pulitzer prize winning poet.
Quoted on page 77

Rohn, Jim
Author and motivational speaker.
Quoted on page 20

Rolland, Romain (1866 - 1944)
French writer and dramatist.
Quoted on page 27

Rumi (1207 - 1273)
Persian poet, Islamic jurist and Hanafi theologian.
Quoted on page 17

Ruskin, John (1819 - 1900)
Author, poet, artist and critic.
Quoted on page 54

Saadi (1184 - 1283)
One of the major Persian poets. Recognised for the quality of his writing and the depth of his social thought.
Quoted on page 4

Saint-Exupéry, Antoine de 1900—1944
French writer and aviator. Author of 'The Little Prince'.
Quoted on page 88

Salinger, Jerome David JD. (Born 1919)
American author best know for his novel The Catcher in the Rye.
Quoted on page 71

Saotomi, Mitsugi (Born 1937)
Japanese Aikido master.
Quoted on page 31

Schrödinger, Erwin (1887 - 1961)
American— Irish physicist famous for his contribution to quantum physics
Quoted on page 69

Schweitzer, Albert (1875 - 1965)
Alsatian theologian, musician, philosopher and physician. Winner of the Nobel Peace Prize.
Quoted on page 97

Serbian proverb
Quoted on page 84

Shaby, Aboodi
Quoted on page 15

Shaw, George, Bernard (1856—1950)
Irish playwright and socialist
Quoted on page 29

Shekerjian, Denise
US author on creativity
Quoted on page 96

Sheng-Yen (Born 1931)
Famous Japanese Zen Buddhism teacher.
Quoted on page 84

Spence, Gerry (Born 1929)
Renowned US trial lawyer.
Quoted on page 64

Spender, Stephen Sir (1909 - 1995)
English poet, novelist and essayist who concentrated on themes of social injustice and
class struggle.
Quoted on page 93

Starr, Pamela Vaull (1909 - 1993)
Poet, artist and writer.
Quoted on page 48

Suenens, Cardinal L.J. Leo Josel (1904 - 1996)
Belgian prelate of the Roman Catholic Church.
Quoted on page 60

Szent-Györgyi, Albert (1893 - 1986)
Hungarian winner of the Nobel Prize in Physiology.
Quoted on page 11

Taylor, Jim
Quoted on page 61

Thornley, Kerry (1938 - 1998)
Co-founder of Discordianism. Co-author of Principia Discordia.
Quoted on page 91

Tyger, Frank
Quoted on page 76

Ueland, Brenda (1891 - 1985)
Journalist, editor, freelance writer and teacher of writing.
Quoted on page 100

Vallett, Robert
Quoted on page 75

Van Gogh, Vincent (1853 - 1890)
Dutch post-impressionist artist.
Quoted on page 16

Watts, Alan (1915 - 1973)
Philosopher, writer, speaker and student of comparative religion.
Quoted on page 87

Wilder, Laura, Ingalls (1867 - 1957)
American authoress of children's books including The Little House on the Prairie.
Quoted on page 70

Winkler, Henry (Born 1945)
Golden Globe winning actor, director, producer and author.
Quoted on page 78

Yamada, Kobi
Writer
Quoted on page 68

Yogananda, Paramhansa (1893 - 1952)
Indian yogi and guru and author of Autobiography of a Yogi
Quoted on page 91

About the Author

Steve Unwin is a Chartered Engineer who, after many years in industry, turned his systems thinking to explore how organisations and people work.

He played a key role in the transformation of the UK based Aerospace business and in 1999 he jointly received the prestigious UK Excellence Award from HRH The Princess Royal in recognition of this work.

In 2001 he left business to focus on the challenge individuals and organisations face when creating improvement.

He is recognised as an insightful and inspiring speaker having appeared at conferences in places as diverse as Khartoum, Tehran, Antwerp and Nepal.

Steve has created several other books which explore the nature of change for individuals and organisations.

Steve lives in Preston in the UK with his family of three children.

To find out more please visit www.steveunwin.com and www.photonbooks.com

Letting go - Take control by letting go

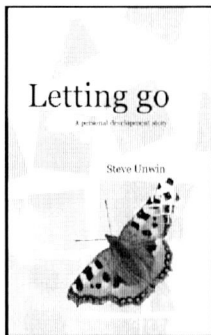

Letting go is a book for anyone facing change, a package of insights to help reshape your understanding.

Real change happens not through what we do, but who we become. Change who we are, and there is no turning back and nothing can remain the same.

In Letting go we explore the universal truths and challenges, and share the fears and the exhilaration that real change can bring. Illuminated with over 80 apposite quotations.

Travellers - A world of questions or answers

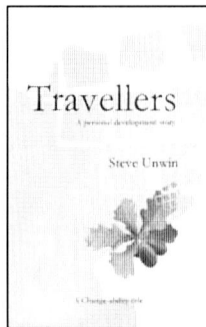

We see things not as they are, but as we are.

'Travellers' explores the contrast between a world seen through questions and one seen through answers. It reveals the impact of the different paradigms we may inhabit and through which we see and understand our world.

Complete with over 80 carefully selected quotations to stimulate new trains of thought, this is a catalyst for change.

For news of these and other exciting titles, please visit www.photonbooks.com

Essence of Da Vinci - Keys to Creativity

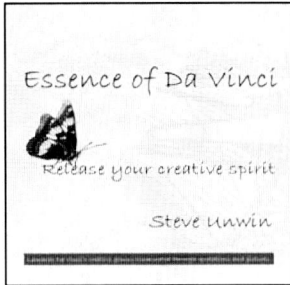

Inspired by Leonardo Da Vinci's thinking style, this insightful and wide ranging collection of quotations, from a wide range of sources, illuminates creative genius in all walks of life.

This is a book that will inspire the creative soul that lurks within all of us.

Featuring over 100 drawings and 250 quotations this is a treasury of insightful prompts to a more creative life.

Himalayan Odyssey - Inspiration from Nepal.

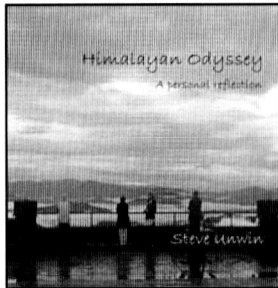

A collection of thought provoking quotations and sketches inspired by a gathering of special people in the Himalayan mountains of Nepal.

With delegates from 15 countries, 'Asian Camp' shared and explored the latest ideas on creating successful change. Himalayan Odyssey enchantingly captures the spirit of the gathering. With nearly 100 quotations and over 100 specially created drawings, it shares and inspires new thinking and change.

For news of these and other exciting titles, please visit www.photonbooks.com

Prague Inspired - City of a thousand spires

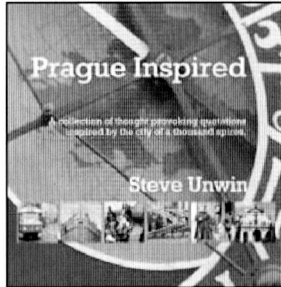

A collection of inspirational quotations and drawings capturing the spirit of the wonderful city of Prague. Venue for Changes of Europe 2008, Prague is a city steeped in change. Be inspired by the architecture, art and magic of this wonderful place.

Contains over 100 carefully selected quotations and drawings. New things to see, to inspire new ways of seeing.

Beyond Best Practice - available Autumn 2008

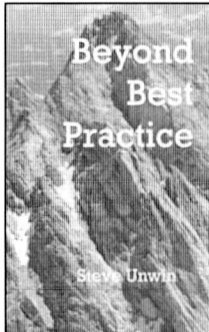

'.... all your knowledge is about the past and all of your questions are about the future.'

In 'Beyond Best Practice' we explore what it takes to survive and succeed in a world where the ground continuously moves from beneath your feet.

For news of these and other exciting titles, please visit www.photonbooks.com